sew practical

13 fun-to-sew designs for you and your home

Martingale®
Create with Confidence

Sew Practical: 13 Fun-to-Sew Designs for You and Your Home
© 2014 by Martingale & Company®

Martingale®
19021 120th Ave. NE, Ste. 102
Bothell, WA 98011-9511 USA
ShopMartingale.com

Printed in China

19 18 17 16 15 14   8 7 6 5 4 3 2 1

Library of Congress Cataloging-in-Publication Data is available upon request.

ISBN: 978-1-60468-386-8

Mission Statement

Dedicated to providing quality products and service to inspire creativity.

Credits

PRESIDENT AND CEO: Tom Wierzbicki
EDITOR IN CHIEF: Mary V. Green
DESIGN DIRECTOR: Paula Schlosser
MANAGING EDITOR: Karen Costello Soltys
ACQUISITIONS EDITOR: Karen M. Burns
TECHNICAL EDITORS: Laurie Baker, Christine Barnes, Nancy Mahoney, and Ellen Pahl
COPY EDITOR: Tiffany Mottet
PRODUCTION MANAGER: Regina Girard
COVER AND INTERIOR DESIGNERS: Paula Schlosser and Connor Chin
PHOTOGRAPHER: Brent Kane
ILLUSTRATORS: Christine Erikson, Adrienne Smitke, and Laurel Strand

Projects in this book have previously appeared in *Cool Girls Quilt; Everyday Handmade; Fig Tree Quilts: Fresh Vintage Sewing; Solids, Stripes, Circles, and Squares;* and *The New Handmade.*

CONTENTS

INTRODUCTION

Those of us who love to sew don't need an excuse to pull out fabrics, books, and notions. The slightest hint of inspiration and a little free time can send us running to our sewing machines to turn out an adorable new purse, a whimsical toy, or a cheery new throw pillow for the sofa.

But who says sewing can't be fun and practical? Instead of a new purse, how about a handy tote bag large enough to carry a dinner party's worth of goodies? And while you're in the kitchen, a pretty apron is a great place to showcase that new fabric you couldn't resist buying. A clever set of place mats can brighten up your kitchen or dining room, or make a wonderful and welcome hostess gift.

Does your sewing space need a makeover? A new sewing-machine cover and sweet pincushion might be just the thing. And if you're a knitter—or your best friend is—the knitting-needle case is a special way to show you care.

You'll find yourself returning again and again to this wonderful collection of timeless designs, and with good reason: great, functional design never goes out of style!

Sew fun, sew pretty, sew practical!

Collector's Item Tote Bag

Designed and made by Adrienne Smitke • Finished size: 12" x 14½" x 2½"

Use your favorite fabrics to make the custom-covered buttons that decorate this simple shopper-style tote. The embroidered grid creates the perfect canvas for showing off your collection. You could also display a selection of antique buttons, 1" pins, or charms. Best of all, once you're finished sewing, this tote is the perfect size to take to the fabric store or the flea market when shopping for additions to your favorite collection.

MATERIALS

Yardage is based on 42"-wide fabric unless otherwise noted.

1 yard of natural linen for bag exterior
1 yard of dark-pink polka-dot cotton fabric for bag lining and straps
2 yards of 20"-wide medium-weight fusible interfacing
20 scraps, at least 3" x 3", of assorted fabrics to cover buttons
20 metal button forms, 1⅛" diameter, and kit for covering buttons*
White embroidery floss
Embroidery hoop (optional)

Adrienne used Dritz button forms, which come with a tool for applying the fabric.

CUTTING

From the natural linen, cut:
1 rectangle, 14" x 16½"
1 rectangle, 13" x 15½"
2 rectangles, 3½" x 15½"
1 rectangle, 3½" x 13"

From the dark-pink polka dot, cut:
2 rectangles, 13" x 15½"
2 rectangles, 3½" x 15½"
1 rectangle, 3½" x 13"
2 strips, 6" x 24"

From the interfacing, cut:
4 rectangles, 13" x 15½"
4 rectangles, 3½" x 15½"
2 rectangles, 3½" x 13"

EMBROIDERING THE BAG

1. With the marking tool of your choice, draw a 7" x 8¾" rectangle centered on the linen 14" x 16½" rectangle. Divide the rectangle into five rows of 1¾" squares, with four squares in each row.

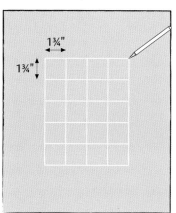

2. Use three strands of white embroidery floss and a running stitch to stitch the marked lines. If you wish, use an embroidery hoop to hold the fabric taut while stitching. Take short, even stitches and tie a knot to secure the loose ends on the back of the fabric.

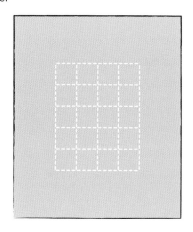

3. Trim the embroidered linen rectangle to 13" x 15½", positioning the grid as shown.

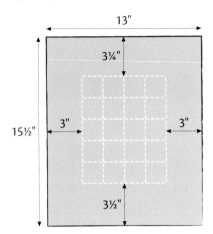

MAKING THE BAG

Use ½"-wide seam allowances unless otherwise indicated.

1. Following the manufacturer's instructions, fuse a 13" x 15½" rectangle of medium-weight interfacing to the wrong side of the embroidered linen rectangle. Repeat with the remaining linen and polka-dot pieces and their corresponding interfacing pieces.

2. With right sides together, stitch a linen 3½" x 15½" rectangle to each long edge of the embroidered rectangle. Stop stitching ½" before the bottom edge, backstitching at the beginning and end of each seam. Press the seam allowances open. Stitch the remaining linen 13" x 15½" rectangle to one edge of the unit.

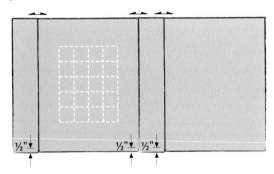

- -

● *Covered-Button Tip*

If you're using thin or gauzy fabrics, fuse a piece of *lightweight* interfacing to the back of the scrap to keep the metal from showing through on the front of the button.

- -

3. Join the remaining lengthwise edges to create a tube, again stopping ½" before the bottom edge. Press the seam allowances open.

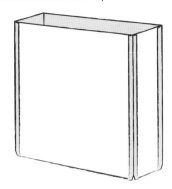

4. With right sides together, pin the linen 3½" x 13" rectangle to the bottom of the tube. Fold the corners up 90° so that the bag sits flat.

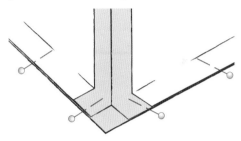

5. Starting in the middle of one long side, stitch around the bottom of the bag. Pivot at each corner, stitch across the point, and backstitch. Trim the corners, making sure not to cut too close to the seam. Turn the bag right side out.

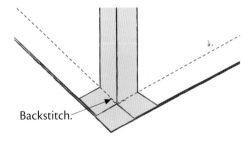

Backstitch.

6. Repeat steps 2 and 3 with the polka-dot 3½" x 15½" rectangles and 13" x 15½" rectangles, leaving a 6" gap along one side seam for turning. Backstitch before and after the gap for extra strength. Repeat steps 4 and 5 to add the polka-dot 3½" x 13" rectangle for the lining bottom, but do not turn the lining right side out.

7. Following the manufacturer's instructions, cover the 20 metal button forms with assorted fabric scraps. Generally, medium-weight fabric or quilting cotton works best. Arrange the buttons on the stitched grid, centering each button in a square. When you are happy with the placement, hand sew the buttons to the bag with white embroidery floss, knotting the tails on the back of the fabric.

8. To make the straps, fold a polka-dot 6" x 24" strip in half *lengthwise*, wrong sides together, and press. Open the strip and turn the raw edges in to meet the fold. Refold, enclosing the raw edges, and press. Topstitch a scant ⅛" from each edge. Make two straps.

Metal button forms for covering are available at your local crafts or fabric store.

ASSEMBLING THE BAG

1. Pin the straps 1½" from either edge on both the front and back of the bag exterior.

2. With right sides together, slip the bag exterior inside the bag lining, sandwiching the straps between the layers and making sure they aren't in the seam allowances. Align and pin or clip (with metal hairclips) the top raw edges together. Sew around the top of the bag, backstitching over the seams and straps.

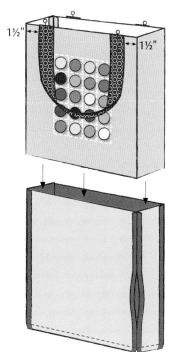

3. Turn the bag right side out by pulling it through the gap in the lining. Whipstitch the gap closed.

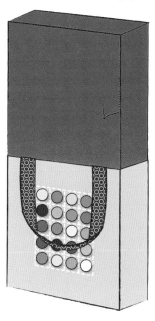

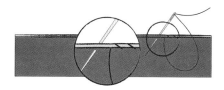

4. Push the lining inside the bag exterior, roll the top edge seam (see "Rolled Seams," page 17), and press the bag. Topstitch ¼" from the upper edge.

Dogwood Blossom Knitting-Needle Case

Designed and made by Adrienne Smitke • Finished size: 6" x 10" when folded

This pretty case has pockets for 16 sets of double-pointed knitting needles up to 7" long, four sets of circular knitting needles, and there's even a smart little zippered pouch for notions built right in. Now you'll always have the right-sized needles on hand. This case would also be perfect for crochet hooks or colored pencils, making it a great gift for your favorite crafter.

MATERIALS

Yardage is based on 42"-wide fabric.

1 yard of teal floral for case exterior, interior flap, and binding

¾ yard of aqua herringbone print for case lining

½ yard of teal polka dot for needle pockets and zippered pouch exterior

½ yard of aqua-and-white print for needle pockets and zippered pouch lining

½ yard of fusible batting

1 yard of 1½"-wide brown woven ribbon for ties

7" zipper

Painter's tape or removable fabric marker

CUTTING

From the teal floral, cut:

1 rectangle, 10" x 12¾"

1 rectangle, 6¾" x 10"

1 rectangle, 12¾" x 14½"

2 strips, 2½" x 42"

From the teal polka dot, cut:

4 rectangles, 7" x 10½"

1 rectangle, 1¾" x 8¼"

1 rectangle, 3¾" x 8¼"

1 rectangle, 5½" x 8¼"

From the aqua herringbone print, cut:

2 rectangles, 7" x 10"

1 rectangle, 6¾" x 10"

From the aqua-and-white print, cut:

4 rectangles, 5¾" x 7"

1 rectangle, 1¾" x 8¼"

1 rectangle, 3¾" x 8¼"

1 rectangle, 5½" x 8¼"

From the fusible batting, cut:

1 rectangle, 10" x 18½"

From the brown ribbon, cut:

2 pieces, 18" long

MAKING THE CASE EXTERIOR

Use ½"-wide seam allowances unless otherwise indicated.

1. Pin the floral 10" x 12¾" and 6¾" x 10" rectangles right sides together along their 10" sides. Find the center of this edge and insert a piece of the ribbon between the two pieces of fabric, aligning the raw edges. Sew the pieces together, backstitching over the ribbon for strength. Press the seam allowances open.

2. Following the manufacturer's instructions, fuse the batting rectangle to the wrong side of the unit made in step 1. Set it aside.

MAKING THE POCKETS

1. Fold each of the polka-dot 7" x 10½" rectangles in half, right sides together, so they measure 7" x 5¼". Stitch the long raw edges opposite the fold on each piece.

2. Finger-press the seam allowances open, turn the pockets right side out, roll the seams (see "Rolled Seams," page 17), and press flat. Topstitch a scant ⅛" from the fold on each pocket.

3. Layer a polka-dot pocket on a herringbone-print 7" x 10" rectangle, right side up, so the pocket seam is 2¼" from the lower edge of the rectangle. Topstitch the pocket to the lining a scant ⅛" from the bottom seam, backstitching at the beginning and end. Make two.

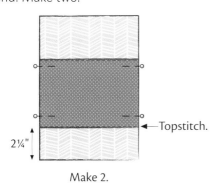

Make 2.

4. Pin a second polka-dot pocket on top of the first so the pocket seam is ¾" from the lower edge of the rectangle. Topstitch the pocket to the lining a scant ⅛" from the bottom seam, backstitching at the beginning and end. Make two.

5. To divide the pockets, use painter's tape or a removable marking tool to mark both sets of pockets as shown. Topstitch on the marked lines, backstitching at the beginning and end.

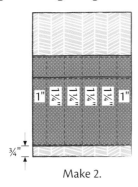

Make 2.

6. Pair two aqua-and-white 5¾" x 7" rectangles right sides together. Using a removable marking tool, mark ½" from the upper-left corner and 2" from the upper-right corner. Connect the marks and stitch on the line. Trim ½" beyond the seam. Make one and one reversed.

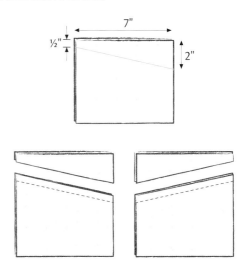

7. Press the seam allowances open, turn the pockets right side out, roll the seams, and press flat. Topstitch a scant ⅛" from the angled edges.

8. Pin the aqua-and-white pockets on top of the polka-dot pocket units made in steps 3 and 4, aligning the bottom raw edges. Mark the center line of each pocket. Topstitch on the marked lines, backstitching at the beginning and end.

9. Trim only the unit on the right to 6¾" wide.

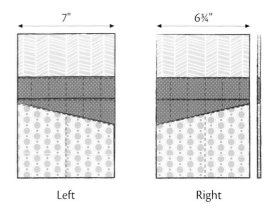

Left   Right

10. With right sides together, pin and sew the two pocket units along the center edges. Press the seam allowances open.

MAKING THE ZIPPERED POUCH

1. Align the zipper, right side up, along the upper edge of the aqua-and-white 1¾" x 8¼" rectangle, also right side up. Align the polka-dot 1¾" x 8¼" rectangle, wrong side up, over the zipper and the lining. Pin.

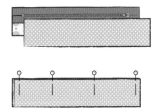

2. Using a zipper foot and a ¼" seam allowance, sew through all layers. Move the zipper pull as needed to make stitching along the zipper easier. Press the fabrics away from the zipper using low heat and the point of your iron.

3. Repeat steps 1 and 2 with the 3¾" x 8¼" rectangles on the other side of the zipper.

4. Topstitch a scant ⅛" from the seams on either side of the zipper.

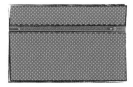

5. Layer the aqua-and-white 5½" x 8¼" rectangle, right side up; the zipper unit you just sewed, also right side up; and the polka-dot 5½" x 8¼" rectangle, wrong side up, as shown, aligning the raw edges. Stitch around the sides and top of the pouch, leaving the bottom open for turning.

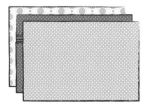

6. Clip the corners, turn the pouch right side out, roll the seams, and press, being careful to avoid the zipper.

ASSEMBLING THE CASE

1. Center the zippered pouch, right side up, along the edge of the herringbone-print 6¾" x 10" rectangle, also right side up. Pin.

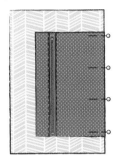

2. Right sides together and raw edges aligned, stitch the unit made in step 1 to the left edge of the pocket unit. Press the seam allowances open.

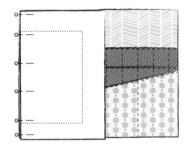

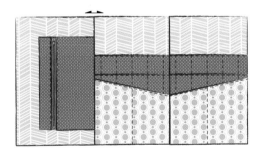

3. To make the flap, fold the floral 12¾" x 14½" rectangle in half, right sides together, so it measures 12¾" x 7¼". Stitch both short sides. Clip the corners, turn the flap right side out, roll the seams, and press. Topstitch a scant ⅛" from the fold.

4. Layer the case exterior and lining panel wrong sides together, with the batting sandwiched in between. Center the remaining piece of ribbon on the left edge of the lining panel. Pin the flap so its top raw edges match those of the lining, and the left edge matches the seam of the zippered pouch. Pin the entire unit with safety pins. Using a long stitch, baste the perimeter a scant ¼" from the edges, backstitching on either side of the ribbon.

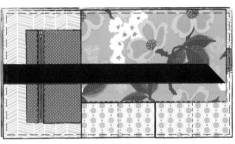

5. Bind the edges using the floral 2½"-wide strips.

Dinner Party Grocery Bag

Designed and made by Cassie Barden • Finished Size: 12" x 13"

With its water- and mess-resistant oilcloth lining, this roomy tote makes a perfect grocery bag, and the version with pockets would make a great diaper bag. It also stands up quite nicely by itself, which all combined makes it a cut above your average brown paper bag or canvas tote. The securely stitched nylon straps let you really load it up. If you crave a bit more organization in your carryalls, instructions for including inside pockets appear on page 16.

MATERIALS

Yardage is based on 42"-wide fabric.

⅞ yard of home-decor or canvas fabric for bag exterior

⅞ yard of coordinating oilcloth or vinyl-coated fabric for bag lining

2⅝ yards of 1"- or 2"-wide nylon or cotton webbing for straps

6¾" x 11¾" piece of book board or plywood* (no thicker than ³⁄₁₆")

Book board is available at paper and art supply stores. Use a large X-Acto knife or mat knife on an old cutting mat to cut book board and a handsaw or power saw to cut the plywood.

CUTTING

From the canvas, cut:
2 rectangles, 13" x 14"
2 rectangles, 8" x 14"
1 rectangle, 8" x 13"

From the lining fabric, cut:
2 rectangles, 13" x 14"
2 rectangles, 8" x 14"
1 rectangle, 8" x 13"
1 rectangle, 12¾" x 14½"

MAKING THE BAG

Use ½"-wide seam allowances unless otherwise indicated.

1. Cut the webbing in half crosswise to make two equal lengths.

2. On the right side of a canvas 13" x 14" rectangle, make marks 2½" in from both bottom corners. With the raw edges aligned along the bottom edge and the outside edge aligned with the marks, pin one webbing length to the fabric so it forms a loop at the top. Repeat with the remaining webbing piece and 13" x 14" rectangle.

3. Using matching thread, sew the straps in place along the outer and inner edges, stopping 1" from the top of the rectangles and backstitching at the beginning and end.

4. With right sides together, sew the canvas 8" x 14" rectangles to each long edge of one strap rectangle from step 3, ending ½" before the bottom raw edge. Add the remaining strap rectangle to the end of this unit, and then join the remaining lengthwise edges to create a tube, again stopping ½" before the bottom edge. Turn wrong side out and press the seam allowances open.

5. With right sides together, pin the canvas 8" x 13" rectangle to the bottom of the tube. Fold the corners up 90° so that the bag sits flat.

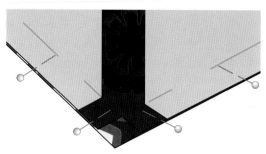

Variation: Adding Inside Pockets

Adding pockets to the inside perimeter of the bag before you sew the bag pieces together is really easy, and you'll only need an additional ½ yard of your lining fabric. You can also sew the pockets to the outside of the bag if you prefer. The pockets will add bulk to all but your top seam, however, so you might try a version without pockets first to get the hang of sewing on the bottom panel.

In addition to the pieces you've already cut (page 15), from the lining fabric, cut:
2 rectangles, 13" x 17"
2 rectangles, 8" x 17"

1. Fold each pocket piece in half along the long edges, wrong sides together, to make pieces 8½" tall.

2. Using matching thread, topstitch ¼" from the fold of each pocket piece.

3. Layer the pocket pieces on the right sides of each lining piece, excluding the bottom. Match the bottom raw edges.

4. Follow the instructions for making the bag, adding the pockets in the side and bottom seams. Don't forget to leave an 8" gap in the lining so you can turn the bag right side out.

6. Starting in the middle of one long side, stitch around the bottom of the bag. At each corner, take two or three extra stitches across the pivot point. Turn the bag right side out.

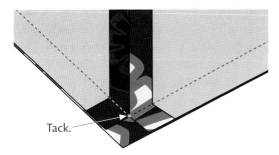

Tack.

7. Repeat step 4 with the lining 13" x 14" rectangles and 8" x 14" rectangles, leaving an 8" gap along one long edge for turning. You will eventually pull the entire bag through this hole, so make sure to backstitch before and after the gap for extra strength. Repeat steps 5 and 6 to add the 8" x 13" rectangle for the lining bottom, but do not turn the lining right side out. When pinning oilcloth or vinyl-coated fabric, pin within the seam allowances so the resulting holes won't show.

8. With right sides together, slip the bag exterior inside the bag lining, sandwiching the straps between the layers and making sure they aren't in the seam allowances. Align the top raw edges and "pin" them together—use metal hair clips for this seam, except around the corners where pins are helpful in matching the corner seams more accurately. Sew around the top of the bag.

9. Turn the bag right side out by pulling it through the gap you left in the lining. Whipstitch the gap closed.

10. Roll the seam along the top edge as well as you can (see "Rolled Seams," right) and use clips to secure it. You'll find that rolling the seams isn't as easy with oilcloth, but with some fussing you can get the seam quite neat. Using matching thread, topstitch ½" from the upper edge of the bag, backstitching over the handles.

Rolled Seams

To achieve clean-finished seams, "roll" them. Sometimes hard-to-iron seams look curled or puffy—as when you're attaching the lining of a bag to the bag exterior and turned it right side out. To smooth out the seam, literally roll the seam on a flat surface, such as an ironing board, cutting mat, or even your pant leg, so that the top fabric rolls slightly to the inside. The more the fabric sticks to the surface, the better. You want the bottom fabric to "grab" the flat surface as your fingers roll the top fabric forward. Give it a try; it's worth the effort to get a wonderful finished edge.

11. To create the insert, fold the lining 12¾" x 14½" rectangle in half, right sides together, to make a 12¾" x 7⅜" rectangle. Sew around one short and the long raw edge using a ¼"-wide seam allowance. Clip the corners and turn the rectangle right side out.

12. Slide the book board or plywood into the lining rectangle from step 11, pushing it all the way to the end. Turn under the seam allowances of the opening and whipstitch the opening closed. Place the insert in the bottom of the bag. It should fit snugly, but if you want a more secure hold, affix a few pieces of self-adhesive Velcro to the insert and the bag bottom.

Curling-Iron Cozy

Designed and made by Barbara Groves and Mary Jacobson of Me and My Sister Designs
Finished size: 5¾" x 14½"

This easy project is perfect for a friend who travels. The Curling-Iron Cozy does double duty to store a curling iron at home! With the cozy's thermal batting, you'll no longer need to set your warm curling iron out to cool near the bathroom sink. Just place it in this handy case and keep the clutter off the bathroom countertop.

MATERIALS

Fat quarters are approximately 18" x 21".

1 fat quarter of print for exterior
1 fat quarter of coordinating print for interior
12" x 15" piece of thermal batting*
2 large coordinating buttons
Embroidery floss for tying buttons
Basting spray

Use a heat-resistant batting, such as Insul-Bright from the Warm Company.

CUTTING

From *each* of the fat quarters, cut:
1 rectangle, 12" x 15" (2 total)

MAKING THE COZY

1. Using the basting spray, generously spray one side of the 12" x 15" piece of thermal batting. Be sure to do this outside in a well-ventilated area. Spraying the batting eliminates slipping and allows you to quilt the pieces later without pinning or basting.

2. Center and place the sticky side of the thermal-batting piece onto the wrong side of the rectangle for the outside of the cozy. Press together firmly with your hands or lightly press with a cool iron.

3. Quilt this layered rectangle (right side up) as desired. Barbara and Mary stitched simple straight lines that crisscross the rectangle. Start by sewing diagonally from corner to corner. Stitch parallel lines outward at 1" intervals in both directions.

Repeat the process by stitching diagonally from the opposite two corners.

4. Some stretching may occur during quilting, so trim the quilted rectangle to measure 12" x 15".

5. With right sides together, layer the fabric rectangle for the inside of the cozy onto the quilted rectangle. (The batting will be on the bottom.) Using a ¼" seam allowance, stitch around all four sides, leaving a 5" opening along one of the short sides for turning. Backstitch at both ends.

5" opening

6. Trim all excess batting away from the seam allowances and clip the corners. Gently turn the cozy right side out. Turn the raw edges at the opening to the inside, press flat, and pin in place.

7. Topstitch ¼" from the edges around the entire rectangle.

8. With the inside of the cozy facing up, fold the rectangle in half lengthwise so that the rectangle now measures 5¾" x 14½" and the opening that you just sewed closed is at the bottom. The outside of the cozy is now showing.

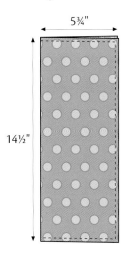

5¾"

14½"

9. Measure 4½" down from the top of the cozy and mark with a pin. Begin sewing at this point, stitching the remainder of the open side and across the bottom, between the outer edge and the previous topstitching line. Backstitch at both ends.

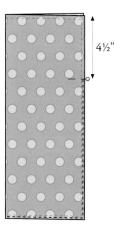

4½"

10. Fold down one of the top flaps to the front of the cozy and attach the buttons with embroidery floss, referring to the photo on page 18 for placement.

Chrysanthemum Sewing-Machine Cover

Designed and made by Linda Lum DeBono • Finished size: 16" x 12" x 7½"

No more vinyl or plastic here! Keep your machine dust-free when it's not in use with this chic design that's sure to inspire.

MATERIALS

Yardage is based on 42"-wide fabric. Fat quarters are approximately 18" x 21".

½ yard of large-scale tan floral for front, back, and binding
⅓ yard of light-blue toile print for gusset
1 fat quarter of light-blue small-scale print for border
Scraps of brown solid for appliqué letters
⅝ yard of brown print for lining
3" x 10" piece of fusible web
3" x 10" piece of stabilizer
24" x 44" piece of batting

CUTTING

All measurements include ¼" seam allowances. The dimensions of each piece below are based on a sewing machine that measures about 15" wide, 12" tall, and 7" deep. Measure your sewing machine and adjust the size of each piece accordingly.

From the light-blue small-scale print, cut:
2 strips, 4½" x 16½"
2 rectangles, 4½" x 8"

From the large-scale tan floral, cut:
2 strips, 2½" x 42"
2 rectangles, 8½" x 16½"

From the light-blue toile print, cut:
1 strip, 8" x 30½"

From the brown print, cut:
2 strips, 12½" x 16½"
1 strip, 8" x 40½"

MAKING THE COVER

1. Following the manufacturer's instructions for the fusible web and using the patterns (page 23) and the brown solid, prepare and cut out the letter shapes. Using the placement diagram (above right), fuse the letters to one light-blue 4½" x 16½" strip.

2. Pin the stabilizer to the back of the strip.

3. Stitch around each letter using a satin stitch and matching thread.

4. Gently remove the stabilizer.

5. To make the front panel, sew the appliquéd strip to one long side of a tan floral 8½" x 16½" rectangle, right sides together. Press the seam allowances toward the floral rectangle. To make the back panel, sew the remaining light-blue strip and tan floral rectangle together; press.

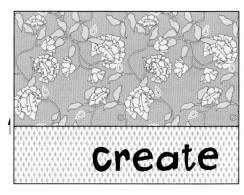

Placement diagram

6. To make the gusset, sew a light-blue 4½" x 8" rectangle to each end of the toile 8" x 30½" strip. Press the seam allowances toward the light-blue rectangles.

7. Cut pieces of batting slightly larger than the front panel, the back panel, and the gusset. Layer each panel and the gusset with batting; baste the layers together. Quilt a curvy, meandering pattern over each piece.

8. Using the curved pattern (page 23), trim both top corners of the front panel and the back panel as shown. Trim any excess batting from all sides of both panels and the gusset.

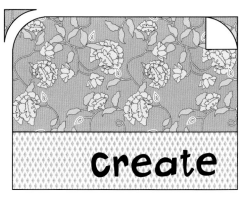

Trim corners.

9. With right sides together, sew the front panel and the gusset together using a ¼" seam allowance. Then sew the back panel to the remaining side of the gusset. Turn the cover right side out.

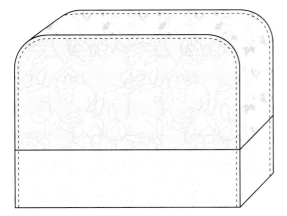

Sew gusset to front and back panels.

ASSEMBLING AND LINING THE COVER

1. Using the curved pattern, trim both top corners of each brown 12½" x 16½" rectangle to make the front and back lining panels.

2. Sew the front and back lining panels to the brown 8" x 40½" strip as you did in step 9 of "Making the Cover" (above), but do not turn the lining right side out.

3. With wrong sides together, tuck the lining inside the cover; pin and stitch a scant ¼" from the raw edges.

4. Using the tan floral 2½"-wide strips, bind the bottom edge.

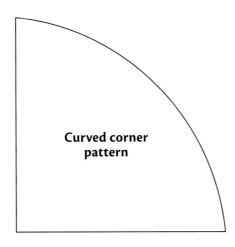

Curved corner pattern

Patterns do not include seam allowances and are reversed for fusible appliqué.

Zinnia Pincushion

Designed and made by Linda Lum DeBono • Finished size: 6½" x 4½" x 3½"

MATERIALS

6" x 15" piece of pink felted wool for flower petals

7" x 9" piece of light-blue felted wool for pincushion sides

7" x 9" piece of lime-green felted wool for pincushion top and bottom

6" x 6" square of moss-green felted wool for leaves

Embroidery floss: cream and colors to match wool and beads

80 light-blue Maco beads for pincushion sides

14 pink cube-shaped beads for flower center

16-ounce bag of polyester fiberfill

Wave fabric shears or wavy-edged rotary-cutting blade for cutting leaves (optional)

CUTTING

All measurements include ¼"-wide seam allowances. Patterns for pieces A–E are on page 26.

From the pink felted wool, cut:
1 *each* of pieces A–D

From the lime-green felted wool, cut:
2 of piece E

From the light-blue felted wool, cut:
2 rectangles, 2½" x 7¼"

ASSEMBLING THE FLOWER

1. Layer the flower shapes A–D, starting with the largest shape on the bottom and ending with the smallest on top.

2. Using a single strand of matching embroidery floss and stitching through all of the layers, sew the pink beads in the center of the flower.

ASSEMBLING THE PINCUSHION

1. Referring to the photo (page 24) and using a single strand of matching embroidery floss, randomly hand sew the blue beads onto each 2½" x 7¼" rectangle.

2. Layer the rectangles with the beaded sides together and, using a ¼" seam allowance, sew along both short ends of the rectangles as shown to make the pincushion side.

What a pretty pincushion to accessorize your sewing space! This is a quick and easy project to make for holiday gifts, and the design possibilities are endless—use different colors of felted wool and other styles of beads for an entirely different look.

3. Fold each lime-green E piece in half lengthwise and lightly crease. Pin one lime-green piece to one edge of the pincushion side, aligning the crease with the side seams of the rectangle. Using two strands of cream-colored embroidery floss, use a hand blanket stitch to sew the pieces together.

Side seam →   ← Side seam

4. Use pattern F (page 26) to cut out three moss-green leaf shapes or use wave fabric shears to make three free-form leaves. Arrange the leaves and the flower on the lime-green top, referring to the photo for placement. Remove the flower; tack the base of each leaf in place by hand. Reposition the flower. Stitching through all the layers, randomly hand stitch through the beads in the flower center to secure the flower to the lime-green top.

5. Repeating step 3, sew the remaining lime-green E piece to the bottom of the pincushion using a blanket stitch. Stop stitching approximately 2" from the starting point to leave an opening for stuffing the pincushion. Firmly stuff the pincushion with polyester fiberfill.

6. Continue sewing a blanket stitch along the bottom of the pincushion to close the opening.

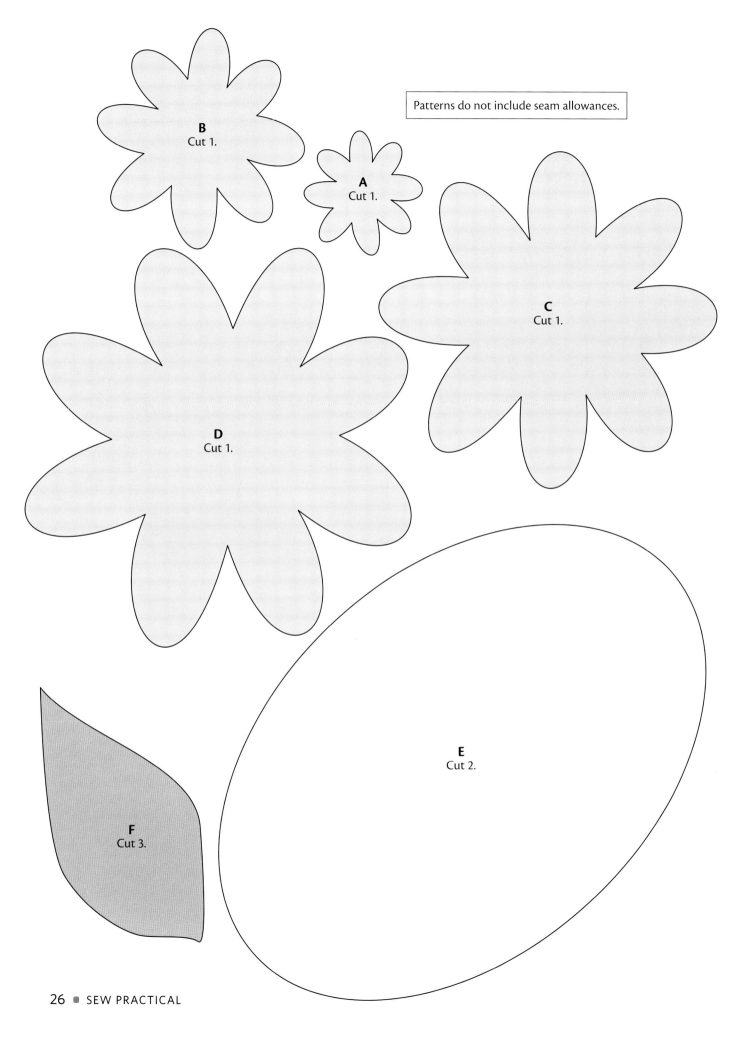

B
Cut 1.

A
Cut 1.

Patterns do not include seam allowances.

C
Cut 1.

D
Cut 1.

E
Cut 2.

F
Cut 3.

Cool Girl's Tool Case

Designed and made by Linda Lum DeBono • Finished size: 9" x 13" when open

A companion to the pincushion on page oo, this tool case is made from gorgeous hand-dyed wools. Pamper yourself by making this carryall to hold all of your little notions. It's a fabulous gift combination with the pincushion—and so fun and fast to whip up.

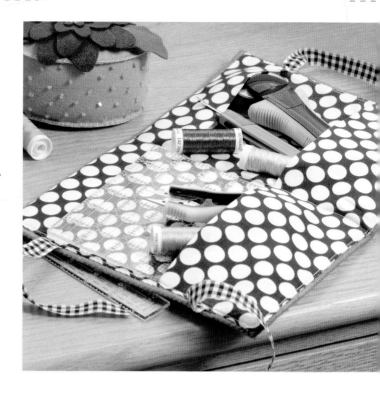

MATERIALS

Yardage is based on 42"-wide fabric.

11" x 15" piece of blue felted wool for cover
5" x 8" piece of red felted wool for flower petals
4" x 6" piece of pink felted wool for flower petals
½ yard of polka-dot print for lining
1 yard of ½"-wide black-and-white checked ribbon
  for ties
9" x 13" piece of heavyweight fusible interfacing
75 lime-green bugle beads for front cover
7 large round pink beads for flower center
Embroidery floss: colors to match wool and beads

CUTTING

*All measurements include ¼"-wide seam allowances.
Patterns for pieces A–D are on page 30.*

From the blue felted wool, cut:
1 rectangle, 10" x 14"

From the polka-dot print, cut:
1 rectangle, 13½" x 22"
1 rectangle, 7½" x 13½"

From the pink and red felted wool, cut:
1 *each* of pieces A–D

From the checked ribbon, cut:
4 strips, 7½" long

ASSEMBLING THE COVER

1. Center the interfacing, adhesive side down, on the wrong side of the blue felted wool rectangle. Following the manufacturer's instructions, fuse the interfacing to the rectangle.

2. Fold the edges of the wool rectangle over the outside edges of the interfacing to the nonadhesive side and press. Use a ¼" seam allowance and a thread color that matches the wool to sew all the way around the outside edge.

3. Layer the flower shapes A–D, starting with the largest on the bottom and ending with the smallest on top. Referring to the placement diagram below, position the layered flower on the front cover. Using a single strand of matching embroidery floss and stitching through all of the layers, including the interfacing, sew the large round beads in the center of the flower.

4. Using a single strand of matching embroidery floss, randomly hand sew the lime-green bugle beads to the front of the cover.

Placement diagram

MAKING THE LINING

1. With right sides together, fold the polka-dot 13½" x 22" rectangle in half as shown and press. Using a ¼" seam allowance, stitch each short end of the rectangle as shown, starting and ending with a backstitch. Leave the long edge open to turn the lining right side out. Turn the rectangle right side out and press.

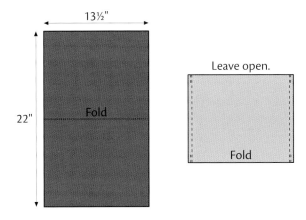

2. Position the rectangle from step 1 with the folded edge at the top. Fold the top folded edge over 1¾" and press.

3. Repeating step 1, fold the 7½" x 13½" rectangle in half lengthwise and stitch each short end of the rectangle. Turn the rectangle right side out and press.

4. Position the smaller rectangle from step 3 on top of the larger rectangle from step 1 to create a pocket, aligning the bottom raw edges of both rectangles together. Machine stitch a scant ¼" from the raw edges.

5. Mark and topstitch a line through the center of the lining. Mark and topstitch evenly spaced lines through the lower section of the lining to form separate pockets.

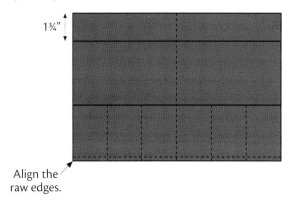

6. Along the bottom edge, turn the seam allowances of the lining under ¼", and press. Using a thread color that matches, sew a scant ¼" from the outer edge around the lining.

7. Place the lining on the cover, covering the wool seam allowance and machine stitches. Tuck the pieces of ribbon between the lining and front cover, two on each side, 2" from the top and bottom edges as shown.

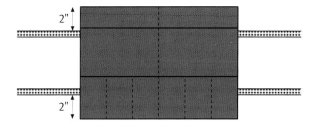

8. Stitch the lining in place using a blind stitch or slip stitch. Then topstitch along the center again, stitching through all the layers to make the spine of the case.

Patterns do not include seam
allowances and are reversed
for fusible appliqué.

C
Cut 1.

B
Cut 1.

D
Cut 1.

A
Cut 1.

Literary Genius E-Reader Cover

Designed and made by Cassie Barden • Finished size: 5½" x 8½" when folded

If you're a gadget geek—or know someone who is—you'll enjoy making and using this handmade case. This clever, simple cover is a great way to protect your e-reader. It feels nice in your hands when you're reading, it's a wonderful showcase for a favorite fabric, and it's quick enough to make that you can outfit all the members of your book club with custom covers of their own.

A NOTE ABOUT SIZES

Measurements for the popular third-generation Amazon Kindle (7.5" tall) and the first and second generations of the Barnes & Noble Nook (7.7" tall) are included. The Nook measurements are shown in brackets. Construction is the same for both readers. If you have a different-sized e-reader, adjust fabric measurements accordingly.

MATERIALS

Yardage is based on 42"-wide fabric unless otherwise noted.

½ yard of turquoise cotton canvas print for case exterior
⅜ yard of purple polka dot for case lining
½ yard of 20"-wide medium-weight fusible interfacing*
Two pieces, 3" long, of ⅜"-wide elastic**
4" length of sew-in ⅝"-wide Velcro

If you use quilting cottons instead of cotton canvas, use a slightly heavier-weight interfacing.

**Match the elastic to the e-reader, not to the fabric.*

CUTTING

From the turquoise cotton canvas print, cut:
1 rectangle, 8¾" x 15" [9" x 15"]
1 rectangle, 3" x 5"
2 squares, 2½" x 2½"

From the purple polka dot, cut:
1 rectangle, 8¾" x 9½" [9" x 9½"]
1 rectangle, 6" x 8¾" [6" x 9"]
1 rectangle, 3" x 5"

From the interfacing, cut:
1 rectangle, 8¾" x 9½" [9" x 9½"]
1 rectangle, 6" x 8¾" [6" x 9"]
1 rectangle, 3" x 5"
2 squares, 2½" x 2½"

MAKING THE CASE

Use ¼"-wide seam allowances unless otherwise indicated.

1. Following the manufacturer's instructions, fuse all but the 2½" squares of fusible interfacing to the wrong side of the corresponding polka-dot pieces. Fuse the small interfacing squares to the wrong side of the corresponding turquoise-print squares.

2. Press each small square in half, wrong sides together, to make a triangle.

3. Pin one piece of elastic to the upper-left corner of the 6" x 8¾" [6" x 9"] polka-dot rectangle, and one folded triangle to the lower-left corner.

1½"

4. With right sides together, stitch the polka-dot 8¾" x 9½" [9" x 9½"] rectangle to the polka-dot 6" x 8¾" [6" x 9"] rectangle along the 8¾" [9"] edges. Press the seam allowances open.

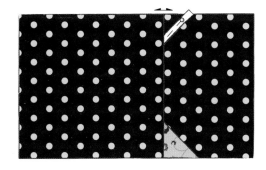

5. Sew the soft (loop) Velcro piece to the polka-dot 3" x 5" rectangle ½" from the right edge and centered vertically.

½"

6. With right sides together, stitch the turquoise-print and polka-dot 3" x 5" rectangles together around three sides, leaving the edge without the Velcro open. Trim the corners, turn the flap right side out, and press.

7. Pin the second piece of elastic to the upper-right corner of the lining. Pin the second triangle to the lower-right corner. Pin the flap to the right edge, lining to lining, with the flap centered vertically.

8. With right sides together and raw edges aligned, pin the turquoise-print 8¾" x 15" [9" x 15"] rectangle to the entire lining unit. Stitch around the perimeter, leaving a 4" gap along the lower-left edge (the area away from the triangles) and backstitching at the beginning and end.

9. Clip the corners, turn the case right side out, and roll the seams (see "Rolled Seams," page 17). Turn under the seam allowances of the opening, press, and pin close to the edge.

10. Place your e-reader in the case. Don't worry if it's a bit loose; just center it within the triangle pockets and elastic. Now fold over the left edge to create the vertical pocket, and then fold again over the reader. Adjust the pocket until everything lines up along the right edge and the corners look square. Pin the pocket to hold it temporarily, and then place a pin at the top and bottom of the vertical fold to mark it.

11. Pin the rough (hook) piece of Velcro to the front cover so it corresponds to the Velcro on the flap. Unfold the cover and remove the e-reader. Stitch the Velcro strip.

12. Refold the pocket, using the pins from step 10 as a guide, and pin. Topstitch a scant ⅛" around the cover perimeter, including the flap.

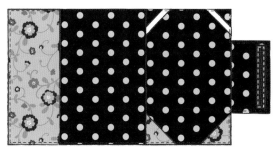

"Charming" Waist Apron

Designed and made by Janis Stob and Margaret Linderman for Fig Tree & Co. • Finished size: 22" x 24", excluding ties

This waist-tied apron is made from scraps of all kinds—it's the perfect clean-up-the-sewing-room project! Charm squares are an easy and precoordinated choice, but any grouping of squares from your stash will look wonderful in this easy apron. Reminiscent of your grandma's kitchen, this simple project can be whipped up on a weekend afternoon and ready for cooking on Monday!

MATERIALS

Yardage is based on 42"-wide fabric. Fat quarters are approximately 18" x 21".

1 yard of muslin for lining
½ yard *total* of assorted fabrics for waistband/ties
24 squares, 5" x 5", of assorted fabrics for pieced front
⅛ yard of fabric for front bottom band
1 fat quarter of coordinating print for pocket
¼ yard of 1"-wide flat lace
1"-diameter button

CUTTING

All measurements include ¼"-wide seam allowances.

From the fabric for the front bottom band, cut:
1 strip, 4½" x 27½"

From the fat quarter for the pocket, cut:
2 squares, 8½" x 8½"

From the lace, cut:
1 piece, 27½" long
1 piece, 10" long

From the muslin, cut:
1 piece, 22½" x 27½"

MAKING THE APRON

1. Arrange the 5" squares into four rows of six squares each. Sew the squares in each row together. Press the seam allowances in opposite directions from row to row. Sew the rows together. Press the seam allowances in one direction.

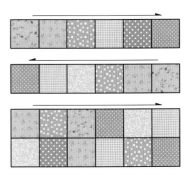

2. With right sides facing up, baste the 27½"-long piece of lace to one long edge of the bottom-band 4½" x 27½" strip. Sew this piece to the step 1 squares, right sides together, with the lace edge aligned with the bottom edge of the pieced squares. Press the seam allowances toward the bottom band.

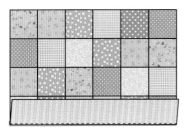

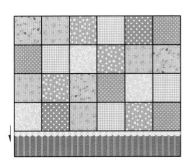

3. To make the pocket, turn under the ends of the 10"-long lace piece ½" and then ½" again; stitch the turned edges in place. Baste the lace to the corner of one of the 8½" pocket squares as shown, pleating as needed to turn the corner.

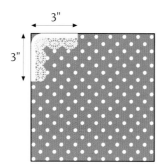

4. Place the remaining pocket square over the lace-trimmed square, right sides together and raw edges aligned. Stitch the squares together, leaving an opening on one of the edges without lace for turning. Turn the pocket right side out and press. Whipstitch the opening closed. Turn down the lace-edged corner and press it in place. Sew the button to the point of the turned-down corner, stitching through all the layers.

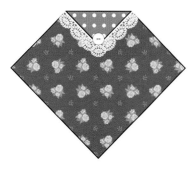

5. Stitch the front and muslin pieces right sides together along the two sides and bottom edge, leaving the top edge open. Turn the apron right side out.

6. Position the pocket on the right-hand side of the apron front on point, with the straight edge of the turned-down corner about 4½" from the top edge

and the side point about 3½" from the apron side. Sew the pocket in place along the edges, leaving the turned-down edge free.

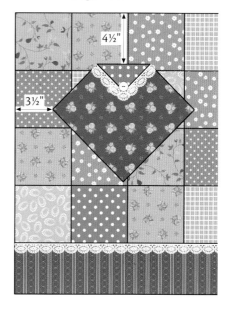

7. Sew two rows of gathering stitches along the top edge of the apron. Evenly gather the top edge to measure 22".

8. To make the waistband, cut the assorted fabrics for the waistband/ties into 2¼"-wide strips of random lengths. Piece them together end to end to make a 124½"-long strip. Press the seam allowances open.

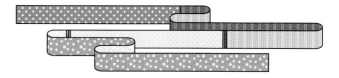

9. With right sides together, sew the ends together to create a circle. Press the seam allowances open. Fold the joined strip in half crosswise at any point; finger-press one of the folds. This will be the center of the strip. Do not turn the piece to the right side.

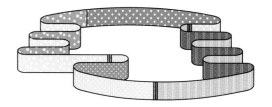

10. Fold the apron in half lengthwise and pin-mark the edge at the fold to mark the center point. With right sides together, place the waistband strip along the top edge of the apron, matching centers. Pin and stitch along this edge. Press the waistband up with the seam allowances pressed toward the waistband. Fold the two ends of the waistband (the tie ends) in half with right sides together, and stitch from the apron edge up and across the top of the waistband tie piece and around to the opposite side as shown. The bottom edge of the back of the waistband will remain open.

Start.   Stop.

11. Turn the waistband ties right side out through the waist opening and press. On the wrong side of the apron, turn under the seam allowances on the open portion of the waistband. Press, and then whipstitch in place through the lining only. Top-stitch ¼" from the edges around the entire waist-band/tie piece.

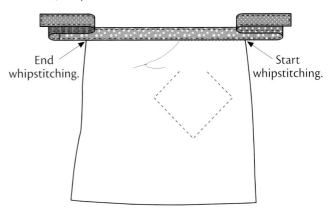

End whipstitching.   Start whipstitching.

Apron Strings Waist Apron

Designed and made by Janis Stob and Margaret Linderman for Fig Tree & Co. • Finished size: 21" x 21", excluding ties

This vertically striped apron combines design elements from a few different vintage aprons. It has a "let's wear this for a skirt" kind of attitude. Try tying one on and see what it does for your attitude!

MATERIALS

Yardage is based on 42"-wide fabric unless otherwise noted.

1 yard of muslin for lining
1 yard of cream polka dot for apron front and ties
¾ yard of red polka dot for apron front
½ yard of coordinating fabric for pocket and waistband
½ yard of contrasting fabric for flanges and binding
⅛ yard of 22"-wide woven fusible interfacing
    (Janis and Margaret used Form-Flex)
Freezer paper

CUTTING

All measurements include ¼"-wide seam allowances. The apron front and lining pieces will be cut after making a template, as described, at right.

From the contrasting fabric for the flanges and binding, cut *on the bias:*
6 strips, 1" x 20", for flanges
1 strip, 1" x 8", for pocket trim
1 strip, 2¼" x 50", for binding*

From the cream polka dot, cut:
2 strips, 6½" x 42"

From the coordinating fabric for the pocket and waistband, cut:
1 strip, 2½" x 42"; cut in half to make 2 strips,
    2½" x 21"
8" circle (A small dessert plate works well for
    a template.)

From the interfacing, cut:
1 piece, 2½" x 21"

*The binding strip can be pieced from two or more lengths of ¼"-wide bias.

CUTTING THE REMAINING PIECES

1. Cut an 8" x 20" piece of freezer paper. Fold the paper in half to make a 4" x 20" piece. With the fold to the left, measure along the top edge 2¼" from the right edge and make a mark. Measure along the bottom edge ½" from the right edge and make another mark. Draw a line to connect the two marks. With the paper still folded, cut on the line. Discard the two pieces that were cut away. Unfold the remaining piece; this is your apron-panel template. Seam allowance is included in this template.

2¼"

½"

2. Use the apron-panel template to cut four pieces from the remainder of the cream polka dot, three pieces from the red polka dot, and seven pieces from the muslin.

ASSEMBLING THE APRON

1. Press each 1" x 20" bias strip in half lengthwise, wrong sides together. Sew to the right-hand edge of three cream polka-dot and three red polka-dot panels. You will have one cream polka-dot panel without a flange.

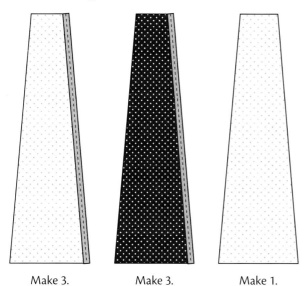

Make 3.   Make 3.   Make 1.

2. Lay out the front panels as shown, alternating colors and ending with the panel without a flange. Sew the panels right sides together along the flange edge in the established order. Press the flange away from the panel to which it was sewn.

🔴 *Stitching the Panels*

When stitching the panels together, follow the stitching line from adding the flange. This will require you to flip the panels over after they are right sides together and sew from the bottom to the top of each piece, but there will be less chance that the previous stitching will show.

3. Sew the seven muslin lining panels together in the same manner as the front panels, omitting the flange detail. Press the seam allowances in the opposite direction as the front panels.

4. Place the front and lining right sides together, aligning the edges. Sew along the sides only, leaving the top and bottom edges open. Turn the apron right side out and press.

5. To make the ties, fold each cream polka-dot 6½" x 42" strip in half lengthwise, right sides together. Trim one end of each strip at a 45° angle. Sew along one long edge and angled end, leaving the straight end open. Turn the strips right side out and press.

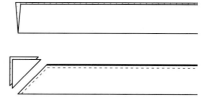

6. Topstitch ¼" from the finished edges of each tie.

7. Following the manufacturer's instructions, fuse the interfacing piece to the wrong side of one of the coordinating 2½" x 21" strips. With the right side of the fused piece facing up, position the straight end of a tie piece on the end of the fused piece, making a small pleat at the straight end of the tie so there is about ½" of space between the sides of the tie and the sides of the waistband. Stitch the tie in place. Repeat on the opposite end of the waistband piece with the remaining tie.

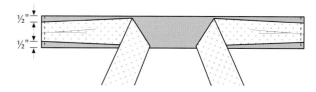

8. Fold the fused waistband piece in half crosswise to find the center; pin-mark the center point along one edge. Fold the apron in half lengthwise to find the center; pin-mark the center point at the top edge.

9. Pin the waistband piece to the front of the apron, right sides together and center points aligned. Stitch the waistband in place along the top edge. Press the waistband up so that the raw edge is now at the top.

10. Press under ¼" along one long edge of the remaining coordinating 2½" x 21" strip. Place this strip over the stitched-on waistband piece, with the pressed-under edge at the bottom and the top edges aligned right sides together. The ties will be sandwiched between the layers. Stitch the pieces together along the ends and top edge.

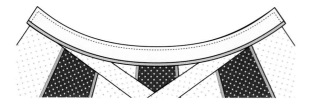

11. Turn the waistband to the right side and press, rolling the seam at the top of the waistband toward the lining side (see "Rolled Seams," page 17). Whipstitch the folded edge to the apron lining on the back side.

FINISHING THE APRON

1. For the pocket, fold the coordinating 8" circle in half and cut along the fold. If necessary, trim the 1" x 8" bias strip to the same length as the cut edge. Fold the bias strip in half lengthwise, wrong sides together. With the raw edges aligned, place the bias strip along the cut edge of one of the pocket halves, right sides together. Place the remaining pocket half over the first, right sides together, sandwiching the bias strip between the layers. Stitch around the pocket, leaving a 1½" opening along one side for turning. Turn the pocket right side out and press the bias strip toward the top of the pocket. Whipstitch the opening closed.

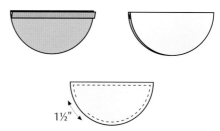

1½"

2. Center the pocket on the third panel (whichever side you prefer) of the apron front, approximately 3¾" from the bottom of the waistband. Stitch the pocket in place along the curved edge, backstitching at the beginning and end to reinforce the pocket corners.

3. Measure the bottom edge of the apron and cut the 2¼" x 50" bias strip 1" longer than the measurement. Fold the strip in half lengthwise, wrong sides together, and press. Stitch the binding strip to the front of the apron along the bottom edge. Press the binding away from the apron. Turn under the excess extending beyond each end ½" so it aligns with the sides of the apron. Fold the binding over the edge and whipstitch it to the apron lining.

Pretty Crafty Apron

Designed and made by Cassie Barden • Finished size: 8½" x 20"

MATERIALS

Yardage is based on 42"-wide fabric.

⅔ yard of large-scale floral for front and back

⅔ yard of small-scale bird print for pocket

½ yard of orange stripe for pocket trim and tie

CUTTING

From the small-scale bird print, cut:
2 strips, 6½" x 21"

From the orange stripe, cut:
2 strips, 6" x 41"
1 strip, 2" x 21"

From the large-scale floral, cut:
2 rectangles, 12½" x 21"

MAKING THE APRON

1. To make the pocket unit, using a ¼" seam allowance and matching the 21"-long edges, sew the orange 2" x 21" strip between the bird-print 6½" x 21" strips. Press the seam allowances open.

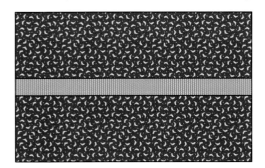

2. Press the pocket unit in half lengthwise, wrong sides together, matching the long raw edges of the bird-print pieces.

3. Layer the pocket unit on the right side of one of the large-scale floral rectangles, matching the bottom raw edges. Mark the pocket sections as shown, using the marking tool of your choice. Sew on the lines through all of the layers using matching or coordinating thread.

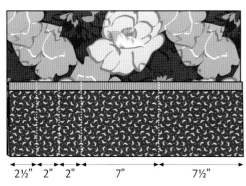

2½"   2"   2"   7"   7½"

4. Layer the remaining large-scale floral rectangle and the pocket unit right sides together, matching the raw edges. Using a ½" seam allowance, sew around the side and bottom edges, leaving the top edge open. Clip the corners, turn the apron right side out, and press.

5. To prepare the tie, sew the two orange 6" x 41" strips together end to end to create an 81"-long strip. Press the strip in half lengthwise, wrong sides together. Unfold and turn the raw edges of the strip in to the center crease. On the ends of the strip, fold the corners in to the center crease at a 45° angle and press. Refold the entire strip on the center crease and press the strip.

6. Fold the apron in half widthwise and finger-press the top raw edge at the center fold. Open up the tie and place it over the top edge of the apron, encasing the raw edge. Match the tie's center seam with the finger-pressed crease of the apron; pin in place. Pin the tie open edges together.

7. Using a scant ⅛" seam allowance, stitch from the open edge of the tie at one end point all the way across the apron and to the opposite end of the tie. This will close the open edges of the tie and attach it to the apron.

Woven Patchwork Place Mats

Designed and made by Pippa Eccles Armbrester • Finished size: 19½" x 15½"

MATERIALS FOR 4 PLACE MATS

Yardage is based on 42"-wide fabric. Fat eighths are approximately 9" x 21".

1 yard *total* of assorted solids *OR* 1 fat eighth *each* of 10 different solids for squares

½ yard of charcoal fabric for vertical strips

½ yard of gray fabric for horizontal strips

1½ yards of solid fabric for backing

¼ yard *each* of 4 different solids for binding: neon green, coral, orange, and blue in the place mats shown

4 pieces of batting, 20" x 24"

CUTTING

From the assorted solids, cut:
80 squares, 3½" x 3½"

From the charcoal fabric, cut:
10 strips, 1½" x 42"

From the gray fabric, cut:
10 strips, 1½" x 42"

From *each* of the 4 fabrics for binding, cut:
2 strips, 2" x 42"

From the fabric for backing, cut:
2 strips, 24" x 42"; crosscut into 4 rectangles, 20" x 24"

ASSEMBLING THE PLACE MATS

Each place mat is composed of four different sections. Mix up the colors of the squares and trim the strips as you go, rather than measuring and cutting them all beforehand. Before pressing the seam allowances, simply trim off the excess strip by cutting along the edge of the square.

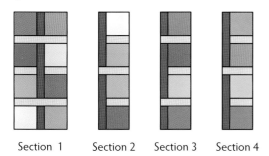

Section 1   Section 2   Section 3   Section 4

Section 1

1. Sew one 3½" square to a charcoal strip. Trim off the excess strip fabric, press the seam allowances open, and sew another 3½" square to the opposite

These simple yet colorful place mats are a great way to jazz up your table for a dinner party, or even an everyday meal, adding character and a celebratory feel no matter the occasion.

side of the strip. Make two of these units with a charcoal strip and two with a gray strip.

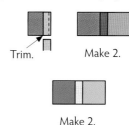

Trim.   Make 2.

Make 2.

2. Sew a gray strip to the long edge of each charcoal unit from step 1. Trim off the excess gray strip.

Make 2.

3. Sew a charcoal strip to the long edge of one gray unit from step 1. Trim off the excess charcoal strip. Sew the remaining gray unit to the other side of the charcoal strip.

4. Sew the units from steps 2 and 3 together as shown to make section 1.

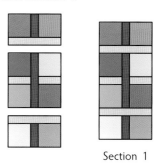

Section 1

Sections 2 and 4

1. Sew two units consisting of two squares, one short gray strip, and a long charcoal strip on one of the

long edges. These units are the same as those created in steps 1 and 2 of section 1, except that the colors of the strips are reversed; the short strip is gray and the long strip is charcoal.

Make 2.

2. Sew a gray strip to the short edge of one of the units from step 1, positioning the long charcoal strip on the left.

Make 1.

3. Sew the units from steps 1 and 2 together as shown to make section 2. Then repeat all steps to make section 4.

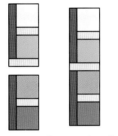

Sections 2 and 4

Section 3

1. Sew a charcoal strip to one side of a square and trim. Make two of these units.

Make 2.

2. Sew together two squares, a short gray strip, and a long charcoal strip as shown. Sew a gray strip to each short edge of the unit, positioning the charcoal strip on the left.

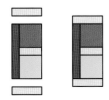

3. Sew the units from steps 1 and 2 together as shown to make section 3.

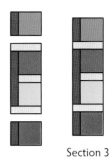

Section 3

Joining the Sections

Sew the sections together, lining up the seams to create the woven effect.

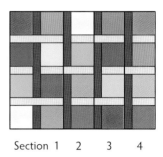

Section 1   2   3   4

FINISHING THE PLACE MATS

1. Baste the place mats and quilt as desired. Pippa free-motion machine stitched a square spiral in each square using beige thread, and an undulating line in the woven strips with matching gray and charcoal thread.

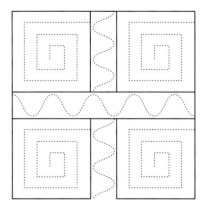

2. Stitch the binding strips for each place mat together to make a continuous strip and bind your place mats.

Pocket Place Mats

Designed and made by Cassie Barden • Finished size: 19" x 14"

A cute addition to the dining room table, a set of these place mats would also be really handy for a picnic. And if you've got kids around at dinnertime, the fun pocket just might make it easier to get help setting the table.

MATERIALS FOR 4 PLACE MATS

Yardage is based on 42"-wide fabric.

2 yards of large-scale blue print for front, back, and pocket

½ yard of dark-red print for pocket background

1 yard of low-loft batting

CUTTING

From the blue print, cut:
4 rectangles, 15" x 20"
4 rectangles, 14" x 15"
4 rectangles, 7" x 12"

From the dark-red print, cut:
4 rectangles, 7" x 15"

From the batting, cut:
4 rectangles, 15" x 20"

MAKING THE PLACE MATS

Use ½"-wide seam allowances throughout.

1. Press a blue 7" x 12" rectangle in half, wrong sides together, to make a 7" x 6" rectangle. Using matching thread, topstitch ¼" along the fold.

2. Position the pocket on a dark-red rectangle, right sides facing up and bottom raw edges aligned. With right sides together, layer a blue 14" x 15" rectangle on top of the pocket piece, matching the short edge of the blue rectangle to the long edge of the pocket piece. Pin along the left edge, and then sew the seam. Press the seam allowances open.

3. Place the front unit and a blue 15" x 20" rectangle right sides together. Place the batting rectangle on top.

4. Sew around the entire piece, using a walking foot if you have one, and leaving a 4" gap along the bottom edge.

5. Turn the place mat right side out through the gap, roll the seams to the back (see "Rolled Seams," page 17), press, and stitch the gap closed.

6. Quilt ¼" around the inside perimeter of the main panel and around the inside perimeter of the pocket panel. If you don't have a walking foot to use for this step, use lots of curved safety pins before you begin stitching to baste the layers together to keep them from shifting. Quilt the main panel within the ¼" border, marking diagonal lines at a 45° angle and 2" apart.

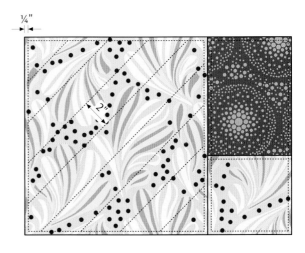